50 Premium Bread Recipes for Home

By: Kelly Johnson

Table of Contents

- Sourdough Bread
- Brioche
- Focaccia
- Ciabatta
- Pain de Campagne
- Challah
- Pain d'épi
- Pretzel Bread
- Panettone
- Multigrain Bread
- Rye Bread
- Olive Bread
- Anadama Bread
- English Muffins
- Bagels
- Pain Poilâne
- Milk Bread
- Irish Soda Bread
- Baguette
- Pumpernickel Bread
- French Pain Complet
- Sweet Cornbread
- Tuscan Bread
- Whole Wheat Sandwich Bread
- Garlic Herb Bread
- Scandinavian Crispbread
- Cinnamon Raisin Bread
- Pane Carasau
- Stuffed Focaccia
- Naan
- Pretzel Rolls
- Dutch Oven Bread

- Soda Bread with Caraway
- Rye with Seeds
- Coconut Bread
- Black Bread
- Oatmeal Bread
- Cheese Bread
- Baghrir (Moroccan Pancake Bread)
- Pain d'épi
- Semolina Bread
- Spelt Bread
- Soft Pretzel Bites
- Kamut Bread
- Kumara (Sweet Potato) Bread
- Sesame Seed Bread
- Olive Oil Bread
- Pane Siciliano
- Herb Focaccia
- Pain au Levain

Sourdough Bread

Ingredients:

- **Starter:**
    - 1 cup (120g) active sourdough starter
    - 1 cup (240ml) warm water
    - 1 cup (120g) all-purpose flour
- **Dough:**
    - 1 ½ cups (360ml) warm water
    - 4 cups (480g) bread flour
    - 2 teaspoons salt

Instructions:

1. **Prepare the Starter:**
    - In a bowl, mix the active sourdough starter with 1 cup warm water and 1 cup flour. Cover and let it sit at room temperature for 4-6 hours, or until it's bubbly and doubled in size.
2. **Mix the Dough:**
    - In a large mixing bowl, combine the starter with the remaining 1 ½ cups warm water. Add 4 cups bread flour and 2 teaspoons salt. Mix until a shaggy dough forms.
3. **Knead the Dough:**
    - Turn the dough onto a floured surface and knead for about 10 minutes until it's smooth and elastic. Alternatively, you can use a stand mixer with a dough hook for this step.
4. **First Rise:**
    - Place the dough in a lightly oiled bowl, cover with a damp cloth, and let it rise at room temperature for 4-6 hours, or until doubled in size.
5. **Shape the Dough:**
    - Punch down the dough to release gas. Shape it into a round or oval loaf, and place it on a parchment-lined baking sheet or in a floured proofing basket.
6. **Second Rise:**
    - Cover the shaped dough with a cloth and let it rise for another 1-2 hours, or until it has roughly doubled in size.
7. **Preheat Oven:**
    - Preheat your oven to 450°F (230°C). If you have a Dutch oven, place it in the oven to preheat as well.
8. **Score and Bake:**
    - Just before baking, use a sharp knife or bread lame to score the top of the dough. This helps control the expansion of the loaf.

- If using a Dutch oven, carefully transfer the dough into it and cover. Bake for 30 minutes, then remove the lid and bake for an additional 15 minutes until the crust is deep golden brown.

9. **Cool:**
    - Let the bread cool on a wire rack before slicing. This allows the interior to set and improves the texture.

Enjoy your homemade sourdough bread!

Brioche

Ingredients:

- **Starter:**
    - 1/4 cup (60ml) whole milk
    - 2 teaspoons active dry yeast
    - 1 tablespoon sugar
- **Dough:**
    - 1/2 cup (115g) unsalted butter, softened
    - 1/2 cup (100g) sugar
    - 1/4 teaspoon salt
    - 3 large eggs, at room temperature
    - 3 cups (360g) all-purpose flour
- **Egg Wash:**
    - 1 large egg
    - 1 tablespoon water

Instructions:

1. **Prepare the Starter:**
    - In a small bowl, warm the milk until it's just lukewarm (not hot). Sprinkle the yeast and sugar over the milk. Stir gently and let it sit for about 5-10 minutes, or until frothy.
2. **Mix the Dough:**
    - In a large bowl or stand mixer, cream the softened butter, sugar, and salt until light and fluffy. Add the eggs one at a time, mixing well after each addition.
    - Gradually mix in the flour and the yeast mixture. Continue mixing until a smooth dough forms. The dough will be slightly sticky.
3. **Knead the Dough:**
    - Turn the dough onto a floured surface and knead for about 10 minutes, or until the dough is smooth and elastic. Alternatively, use the dough hook attachment on a stand mixer.
4. **First Rise:**
    - Place the dough in a lightly greased bowl, cover with plastic wrap or a damp cloth, and let it rise in a warm place for 1-2 hours, or until doubled in size.
5. **Shape the Dough:**
    - Punch down the dough to release gas. You can shape it into a loaf, divide it into smaller portions for individual brioche rolls, or use a brioche mold if you have one.

- For a classic loaf, shape the dough into a rectangle and place it into a greased loaf pan. For rolls, shape the dough into balls and place them in a greased muffin tin or pan.
6. **Second Rise:**
   - Cover the shaped dough with a cloth and let it rise for another 1 hour, or until puffed and nearly doubled in size.
7. **Preheat Oven:**
   - Preheat your oven to 375°F (190°C).
8. **Apply Egg Wash:**
   - Beat the egg with 1 tablespoon of water. Brush this egg wash over the top of the dough for a glossy finish.
9. **Bake:**
   - Bake for 25-30 minutes, or until the brioche is golden brown and sounds hollow when tapped on the bottom. The internal temperature should be around 190°F (88°C).
10. **Cool:**
    - Let the brioche cool in the pan for about 10 minutes before transferring it to a wire rack to cool completely.

Enjoy your rich and buttery brioche!

Focaccia

Ingredients:

- **Dough:**
    - 2 cups (480ml) warm water
    - 1/4 cup (60ml) olive oil, plus more for drizzling
    - 2 teaspoons sugar
    - 1 packet (2 ¼ teaspoons) active dry yeast
    - 5 cups (600g) all-purpose flour
    - 2 teaspoons salt
- **Topping:**
    - 2-3 tablespoons olive oil
    - Coarse sea salt
    - Fresh rosemary or other herbs (optional)

Instructions:

1. **Prepare the Dough:**
    - In a small bowl, combine warm water, sugar, and yeast. Let it sit for 5-10 minutes until foamy.
    - In a large bowl, mix flour and salt. Make a well in the center and add the yeast mixture and 1/4 cup olive oil. Mix until a dough forms.
2. **Knead and Rise:**
    - Turn the dough onto a floured surface and knead for about 10 minutes, until smooth and elastic. Alternatively, use a stand mixer with a dough hook.
    - Place the dough in a lightly oiled bowl, cover, and let it rise in a warm place for 1-2 hours, or until doubled in size.
3. **Shape and Second Rise:**
    - Punch down the dough and transfer it to a greased baking sheet or a 9x13-inch pan. Stretch and press the dough to fit the pan.
    - Cover with a cloth and let it rise for 30 minutes.
4. **Preheat Oven:**
    - Preheat your oven to 450°F (230°C).
5. **Add Toppings:**
    - Dimple the dough with your fingers. Drizzle generously with olive oil, and sprinkle with coarse sea salt and fresh rosemary or other herbs if desired.
6. **Bake:**
    - Bake for 20-25 minutes, or until golden brown.
7. **Cool:**
    - Let it cool slightly before slicing.

Enjoy your homemade focaccia!

Ciabatta

Ingredients:

- **Starter (Biga):**
    - 1 cup (120g) all-purpose flour
    - 1/2 cup (120ml) water
    - 1/4 teaspoon active dry yeast
- **Dough:**
    - 2 1/2 cups (300g) all-purpose flour
    - 1 1/2 teaspoons salt
    - 1 cup (240ml) water
    - 1/2 teaspoon active dry yeast

Instructions:

1. **Prepare the Biga:**
    - Mix the flour, water, and yeast in a bowl until combined. Cover and let it sit at room temperature for 12-16 hours.
2. **Mix the Dough:**
    - In a large bowl, combine the flour, salt, and yeast. Add the biga and water, mixing until a sticky dough forms.
3. **Knead the Dough:**
    - Transfer the dough to a floured surface and gently knead for about 5 minutes. The dough will be quite wet and sticky.
4. **First Rise:**
    - Place the dough in a lightly oiled bowl, cover with plastic wrap, and let it rise for 1-2 hours, or until doubled in size.
5. **Shape the Loaves:**
    - Gently turn the dough onto a floured surface. Divide it into two pieces and shape into long, flat loaves. Transfer to a parchment-lined baking sheet.
6. **Second Rise:**
    - Cover the loaves with a cloth and let them rise for 30-45 minutes.
7. **Preheat Oven:**
    - Preheat your oven to 475°F (245°C).
8. **Bake:**
    - Bake the ciabatta for 25-30 minutes, or until golden brown and crusty.
9. **Cool:**
    - Let the loaves cool on a wire rack before slicing.

Enjoy your airy and crusty ciabatta!

Pain de Campagne

Ingredients:

- 500g (4 cups) bread flour
- 100g (1 cup) whole wheat flour
- 350ml (1½ cups) water
- 100g (½ cup) sourdough starter (active)
- 10g (2 tsp) salt
- 5g (1 tsp) sugar (optional)

Instructions:

1. In a large bowl, mix the bread flour, whole wheat flour, and salt.
2. In another bowl, combine the water, sourdough starter, and sugar (if using).
3. Pour the wet ingredients into the dry ingredients and mix until a rough dough forms.
4. Knead the dough on a floured surface for about 10 minutes until smooth and elastic.
5. Place the dough in a lightly oiled bowl, cover with a damp cloth, and let it rise in a warm place for 2 hours, or until doubled in size.
6. Preheat the oven to 230°C (450°F) with a baking stone or heavy baking sheet inside.
7. Turn the dough out onto a floured surface and shape it into a round or oval loaf.
8. Place the dough on parchment paper and let it rise for another 30-45 minutes.
9. Score the top of the loaf with a sharp knife.
10. Transfer the loaf to the preheated oven and bake for 30-35 minutes, or until the crust is golden brown and the loaf sounds hollow when tapped on the bottom.
11. Let the bread cool on a wire rack before slicing.

Challah

Ingredients:

- 4 cups all-purpose flour
- ½ cup sugar
- 2 tsp salt
- 1 packet (2¼ tsp) active dry yeast
- 1 cup warm water
- ¼ cup vegetable oil
- 3 large eggs
- 1 egg yolk (for egg wash)

Instructions:

1. In a bowl, mix warm water, sugar, and yeast. Let it sit for 5-10 minutes until frothy.
2. In a large bowl, combine flour and salt. Make a well in the center and add the yeast mixture, oil, and 2 eggs. Mix until a dough forms.
3. Knead the dough on a floured surface for about 10 minutes until smooth.
4. Place dough in an oiled bowl, cover, and let rise for 1-2 hours, or until doubled in size.
5. Punch down the dough and divide it into three equal parts. Roll each part into a rope and braid them together.
6. Place the braided loaf on a baking sheet, cover, and let rise for 30-45 minutes.
7. Preheat the oven to 375°F (190°C). Brush the loaf with beaten egg yolk.
8. Bake for 25-30 minutes, or until golden brown and hollow sounding when tapped.
9. Cool on a wire rack before slicing.

Pain d'épi

Ingredients:

- 500g (4 cups) bread flour
- 350ml (1½ cups) warm water
- 100g (½ cup) sourdough starter or 1 packet (2¼ tsp) active dry yeast
- 10g (2 tsp) salt
- 30g (2 tbsp) sugar (optional)
- 30g (2 tbsp) unsalted butter, softened (optional)

Instructions:

1. **Prepare the Dough:**
    - If using active dry yeast, dissolve it and the sugar (if using) in warm water and let it sit for 5-10 minutes until frothy.
    - In a large bowl, mix the bread flour and salt.
    - Make a well in the center and add the yeast mixture (or sourdough starter) and butter (if using). Mix until a dough forms.
    - Knead the dough on a floured surface for about 10 minutes until smooth and elastic.
2. **First Rise:**
    - Place the dough in a lightly oiled bowl, cover with a damp cloth, and let it rise in a warm place for 1-2 hours, or until doubled in size.
3. **Shape the Dough:**
    - Punch down the dough and turn it out onto a floured surface.
    - Divide the dough into 2 equal pieces.
    - Shape each piece into a loaf and then shape them into a stalk of wheat. This is typically done by rolling the dough into a long, tapered shape and making small slashes along the sides to create the appearance of individual wheat grains.
    - Place the shaped loaves on a baking sheet lined with parchment paper.
4. **Second Rise:**
    - Cover the loaves with a damp cloth and let them rise for another 30-45 minutes.
5. **Bake:**
    - Preheat the oven to 375°F (190°C).
    - Optionally, brush the loaves with water for a crispier crust.
    - Bake for 25-30 minutes, or until the loaves are golden brown and sound hollow when tapped on the bottom.
6. **Cool:**
    - Let the Pain d'épi cool on a wire rack before slicing.

Pretzel Bread

Ingredients:

- 4 cups all-purpose flour
- 1 packet (2¼ tsp) active dry yeast
- 1½ cups warm water
- ¼ cup baking soda
- 1 tbsp sugar
- 2 tsp salt
- 1 egg, beaten (for egg wash)
- Coarse sea salt (for topping)

Instructions:

1. **Prepare the Dough:**
    - Dissolve yeast and sugar in warm water and let sit for 5-10 minutes until frothy.
    - In a large bowl, combine flour and salt.
    - Add the yeast mixture and mix until a dough forms.
    - Knead on a floured surface for about 8-10 minutes until smooth.
2. **First Rise:**
    - Place the dough in an oiled bowl, cover with a damp cloth, and let rise in a warm place for 1-2 hours, or until doubled in size.
3. **Shape and Boil:**
    - Punch down the dough and shape it into a loaf or desired shape.
    - Preheat oven to 375°F (190°C).
    - Bring a large pot of water to a boil and add baking soda.
    - Boil the bread for 30 seconds, then remove with a slotted spoon and place on a baking sheet lined with parchment paper.
4. **Bake:**
    - Brush with beaten egg and sprinkle with coarse sea salt.
    - Bake for 25-30 minutes, or until golden brown and sounds hollow when tapped.
5. **Cool:**
    - Let the Pretzel Bread cool on a wire rack before slicing.

Panettone

Ingredients:

- 4 cups all-purpose flour
- ¾ cup sugar
- 1 tsp salt
- 1 packet (2¼ tsp) active dry yeast
- ¾ cup warm milk
- ¼ cup water
- ¼ cup unsalted butter, softened
- 3 large eggs
- 1 tsp vanilla extract
- 1 cup mixed dried fruit (raisins, candied orange peel, etc.)
- ½ cup chopped nuts (optional)
- Zest of 1 orange

Instructions:

1. **Prepare the Dough:**
   - Dissolve yeast in warm milk and water, let sit for 5-10 minutes.
   - In a large bowl, mix flour, sugar, and salt.
   - Add yeast mixture, butter, eggs, and vanilla. Mix until a dough forms.
   - Knead on a floured surface for about 10 minutes until smooth.
2. **First Rise:**
   - Place dough in a lightly oiled bowl, cover, and let rise for 1-2 hours, or until doubled in size.
3. **Add Fruit and Nuts:**
   - Punch down the dough, then knead in dried fruit, nuts, and orange zest.
4. **Shape and Second Rise:**
   - Shape dough into a ball and place in a panettone mold or a high-sided round pan.
   - Let rise for 1 hour, or until it has risen above the rim of the pan.
5. **Bake:**
   - Preheat oven to 350°F (175°C).
   - Bake for 45-60 minutes, or until golden brown and a skewer inserted into the center comes out clean.
6. **Cool:**
   - Cool on a wire rack before slicing.

Multigrain Bread

Ingredients:

- 1 cup warm water
- 2 tbsp honey or maple syrup
- 2 tsp active dry yeast
- 2 cups bread flour
- 1 cup whole wheat flour
- 1 cup mixed grains (such as rolled oats, flaxseeds, sunflower seeds, or millet)
- 2 tbsp olive oil
- 1 tsp salt
- ¼ cup chopped nuts or seeds (optional)

Instructions:

1. **Activate the Yeast:**
    - In a small bowl, combine warm water and honey. Sprinkle yeast over the top and let it sit for 5-10 minutes until frothy.
2. **Mix the Dough:**
    - In a large bowl, combine bread flour, whole wheat flour, and salt.
    - Make a well in the center and add the yeast mixture, olive oil, and mixed grains. Mix until a dough forms.
3. **Knead the Dough:**
    - Turn the dough out onto a floured surface and knead for about 8-10 minutes, or until smooth and elastic. If using nuts or seeds, knead them in during the last few minutes.
4. **First Rise:**
    - Place the dough in a lightly oiled bowl, cover with a damp cloth, and let it rise in a warm place for 1-2 hours, or until doubled in size.
5. **Shape and Second Rise:**
    - Punch down the dough and shape it into a loaf. Place it in a greased loaf pan or shape it into a round loaf and place it on a baking sheet.
    - Cover and let rise for another 30-45 minutes.
6. **Bake:**
    - Preheat the oven to 375°F (190°C).
    - Bake for 30-35 minutes, or until the bread is golden brown and sounds hollow when tapped on the bottom.
7. **Cool:**
    - Let the bread cool on a wire rack before slicing.

Rye Bread

Ingredients:

- 1 cup warm water
- 1 packet (2¼ tsp) active dry yeast
- 1 tbsp sugar
- 1 cup rye flour
- 2 cups bread flour
- 1 tbsp caraway seeds (optional)
- 1 tsp salt
- 2 tbsp olive oil

Instructions:

1. **Activate the Yeast:**
    - Dissolve sugar in warm water, then sprinkle yeast over the top. Let sit for 5-10 minutes until frothy.
2. **Mix the Dough:**
    - In a large bowl, combine rye flour, bread flour, caraway seeds (if using), and salt.
    - Add the yeast mixture and olive oil. Mix until a dough forms.
3. **Knead the Dough:**
    - Turn dough onto a floured surface and knead for about 8-10 minutes, until smooth.
4. **First Rise:**
    - Place dough in a greased bowl, cover with a damp cloth, and let rise for 1-2 hours, or until doubled.
5. **Shape and Second Rise:**
    - Punch down the dough and shape into a loaf. Place in a greased loaf pan.
    - Cover and let rise for 30-45 minutes.
6. **Bake:**
    - Preheat oven to 375°F (190°C).
    - Bake for 30-35 minutes, or until the bread is dark brown and sounds hollow when tapped.
7. **Cool:**
    - Let cool on a wire rack before slicing.

Olive Bread

Ingredients:

- 3 cups all-purpose flour
- 1 cup warm water
- 2 tsp active dry yeast
- 1 tsp sugar
- 1 tsp salt
- ¼ cup olive oil
- 1 cup pitted olives (green or black), chopped
- 1 tbsp chopped fresh rosemary or thyme (optional)

Instructions:

1. **Activate the Yeast:**
   - Dissolve sugar in warm water, sprinkle yeast over, and let sit for 5-10 minutes until frothy.
2. **Mix the Dough:**
   - In a large bowl, combine flour and salt.
   - Add the yeast mixture and olive oil. Mix until a dough forms.
   - Knead in the chopped olives and herbs (if using) until evenly distributed.
3. **Knead the Dough:**
   - Turn dough onto a floured surface and knead for about 8 minutes, until smooth and elastic.
4. **First Rise:**
   - Place dough in a greased bowl, cover, and let rise for 1-2 hours, or until doubled in size.
5. **Shape and Second Rise:**
   - Punch down dough and shape into a loaf or round loaf.
   - Place on a baking sheet and cover. Let rise for 30-45 minutes.
6. **Bake:**
   - Preheat oven to 375°F (190°C).
   - Bake for 30-35 minutes, or until golden brown and hollow-sounding when tapped.
7. **Cool:**
   - Let cool on a wire rack before slicing.

Anadama Bread

Ingredients:

- 1 cup cornmeal
- 1 cup boiling water
- 2½ cups all-purpose flour
- ¼ cup molasses
- 2 tbsp sugar
- 1 packet (2¼ tsp) active dry yeast
- 1 cup warm water
- 2 tbsp unsalted butter, softened
- 1 tsp salt

Instructions:

1. **Prepare the Cornmeal Mixture:**
   - In a bowl, pour boiling water over the cornmeal, stirring until smooth. Let it cool to lukewarm.
2. **Activate the Yeast:**
   - Dissolve sugar in warm water, then sprinkle yeast over the top. Let it sit for 5-10 minutes until frothy.
3. **Mix the Dough:**
   - In a large bowl, combine flour and salt.
   - Add the yeast mixture, molasses, and softened butter to the cooled cornmeal mixture. Stir to combine.
   - Gradually add the flour mixture to the cornmeal mixture, mixing until a dough forms.
4. **Knead the Dough:**
   - Turn dough onto a floured surface and knead for about 8-10 minutes until smooth and elastic.
5. **First Rise:**
   - Place dough in a greased bowl, cover with a damp cloth, and let rise in a warm place for 1-2 hours, or until doubled in size.
6. **Shape and Second Rise:**
   - Punch down the dough and shape it into a loaf.
   - Place in a greased loaf pan, cover, and let rise for 30-45 minutes.
7. **Bake:**
   - Preheat oven to 375°F (190°C).
   - Bake for 30-35 minutes, or until the bread is golden brown and sounds hollow when tapped.
8. **Cool:**

- Let the bread cool on a wire rack before slicing.

English Muffins

Ingredients:

- 1 cup warm milk
- 2 tsp active dry yeast
- 1 tbsp sugar
- 3 cups all-purpose flour
- 1 tsp salt
- 2 tbsp unsalted butter, softened
- Cornmeal (for dusting)

Instructions:

1. **Activate the Yeast:**
   - Dissolve sugar in warm milk, sprinkle yeast over, and let sit for 5-10 minutes until frothy.
2. **Mix the Dough:**
   - In a large bowl, combine flour and salt.
   - Add the yeast mixture and softened butter. Mix until a dough forms.
3. **Knead the Dough:**
   - Turn dough onto a floured surface and knead for about 8 minutes until smooth.
4. **First Rise:**
   - Place dough in a greased bowl, cover, and let rise for 1-1½ hours, or until doubled in size.
5. **Shape and Second Rise:**
   - Punch down the dough and roll it out to about ½-inch thickness.
   - Cut into rounds with a cookie cutter or glass.
   - Place rounds on a cornmeal-dusted baking sheet. Cover and let rise for 30 minutes.
6. **Cook:**
   - Heat a griddle or skillet over medium-low heat.
   - Cook muffins for 5-7 minutes on each side, or until golden brown and cooked through.
7. **Cool:**
   - Let cool on a wire rack before splitting and toasting.

Bagels

Ingredients:

- 1½ cups warm water
- 1 packet (2¼ tsp) active dry yeast
- 1 tbsp sugar
- 4 cups bread flour
- 1½ tsp salt
- 2 tbsp honey or sugar (for boiling)
- 1 egg, beaten (for egg wash)
- Toppings (e.g., sesame seeds, poppy seeds, coarse salt)

Instructions:

1. **Activate the Yeast:**
   - Dissolve sugar in warm water, sprinkle yeast over, and let sit for 5-10 minutes until frothy.
2. **Mix the Dough:**
   - In a large bowl, combine flour and salt.
   - Add yeast mixture and mix until a dough forms. Knead on a floured surface for about 10 minutes, until smooth and elastic.
3. **First Rise:**
   - Place dough in a greased bowl, cover, and let rise for 1 hour, or until doubled in size.
4. **Shape the Bagels:**
   - Punch down the dough and divide into 8-10 pieces.
   - Shape each piece into a ball and poke a hole in the center. Stretch the hole to form a ring.
5. **Boil:**
   - Preheat oven to 425°F (220°C).
   - Bring a large pot of water to a boil, adding honey or sugar.
   - Boil bagels for 1-2 minutes on each side, then drain.
6. **Bake:**
   - Place boiled bagels on a baking sheet lined with parchment paper.
   - Brush with beaten egg and sprinkle with toppings.
   - Bake for 20-25 minutes, or until golden brown.
7. **Cool:**
   - Let bagels cool on a wire rack before slicing.

Pain Poilâne

Ingredients:

- 500g (4 cups) bread flour
- 100g (1 cup) whole wheat flour
- 350ml (1½ cups) water
- 150g (½ cup) active sourdough starter
- 10g (2 tsp) salt

Instructions:

1. **Prepare the Dough:**
    - In a large bowl, mix bread flour, whole wheat flour, and salt.
    - In another bowl, combine water and sourdough starter.
    - Pour the wet ingredients into the dry ingredients and mix until a dough forms.
2. **Knead:**
    - Turn dough onto a floured surface and knead for about 10 minutes until smooth and elastic.
3. **First Rise:**
    - Place dough in a lightly oiled bowl, cover, and let rise for 1-2 hours, or until doubled.
4. **Shape and Second Rise:**
    - Punch down the dough and shape it into a round loaf.
    - Place on a parchment-lined baking sheet or in a proofing basket.
    - Cover and let rise for 1-2 hours.
5. **Bake:**
    - Preheat oven to 450°F (230°C) with a baking stone or heavy baking sheet inside.
    - Optionally, score the top of the loaf.
    - Bake for 35-45 minutes, or until crusty and hollow-sounding when tapped.
6. **Cool:**
    - Let the bread cool on a wire rack before slicing.

Milk Bread

Ingredients:

- 3 cups all-purpose flour
- 1 cup warm milk
- ¼ cup sugar
- 1 packet (2¼ tsp) active dry yeast
- ¼ cup unsalted butter, softened
- 1 tsp salt
- 1 large egg

Instructions:

1. **Activate the Yeast:**
   - Dissolve sugar in warm milk, sprinkle yeast over, and let sit for 5-10 minutes until frothy.
2. **Mix the Dough:**
   - In a large bowl, combine flour and salt.
   - Add the yeast mixture, butter, and egg. Mix until a dough forms.
3. **Knead the Dough:**
   - Turn dough onto a floured surface and knead for about 8-10 minutes, until smooth and elastic.
4. **First Rise:**
   - Place dough in a greased bowl, cover, and let rise for 1-1½ hours, or until doubled.
5. **Shape and Second Rise:**
   - Punch down dough and shape into a loaf or divide into smaller pieces for rolls.
   - Place in a greased loaf pan or on a baking sheet. Cover and let rise for 30-45 minutes.
6. **Bake:**
   - Preheat oven to 350°F (175°C).
   - Bake for 25-30 minutes, or until golden brown and a toothpick inserted into the center comes out clean.
7. **Cool:**
   - Let cool on a wire rack before slicing.

Irish Soda Bread

Ingredients:

- 4 cups all-purpose flour
- 1 tsp baking soda
- 1 tsp salt
- 1¼ cups buttermilk

Instructions:

1. **Preheat Oven:**
   - Preheat oven to 425°F (220°C).
2. **Mix Dry Ingredients:**
   - In a large bowl, whisk together flour, baking soda, and salt.
3. **Add Buttermilk:**
   - Make a well in the center of the dry ingredients and pour in the buttermilk.
   - Stir until a rough dough forms; do not overmix.
4. **Shape and Score:**
   - Turn the dough onto a floured surface and shape into a round loaf.
   - Place on a baking sheet and score an "X" on the top with a knife.
5. **Bake:**
   - Bake for 30-35 minutes, or until the bread is golden brown and sounds hollow when tapped.
6. **Cool:**
   - Let cool on a wire rack before slicing.

Baguette

Ingredients:

- 3½ cups all-purpose flour
- 1½ cups warm water
- 1 packet (2¼ tsp) active dry yeast
- 2 tsp salt
- 1 tbsp sugar (optional)

Instructions:

1. **Activate Yeast:**
   - Dissolve sugar in warm water, sprinkle yeast over, and let sit for 5-10 minutes until frothy.
2. **Mix Dough:**
   - Combine flour and salt in a large bowl.
   - Add the yeast mixture and mix until a dough forms.
3. **Knead:**
   - Turn dough onto a floured surface and knead for about 10 minutes, until smooth and elastic.
4. **First Rise:**
   - Place dough in a greased bowl, cover, and let rise for 1-2 hours, or until doubled in size.
5. **Shape and Second Rise:**
   - Punch down dough and divide into 2-3 pieces.
   - Shape each piece into a long, thin loaf and place on a baking sheet lined with parchment paper.
   - Cover and let rise for 30-45 minutes.
6. **Preheat Oven:**
   - Preheat oven to 475°F (245°C). Place a shallow pan of water on the bottom rack for steam.
7. **Bake:**
   - Slash the tops of the loaves with a sharp knife.
   - Bake for 20-25 minutes, or until golden brown and crisp.
8. **Cool:**
   - Let cool on a wire rack before slicing.

Pumpernickel Bread

Ingredients:

- 1¼ cups warm water
- 1 packet (2¼ tsp) active dry yeast
- 2 tbsp molasses
- 1 cup coarsely ground rye flour
- 1 cup all-purpose flour
- ½ cup whole wheat flour
- 2 tbsp cocoa powder
- 1 tbsp caraway seeds (optional)
- 1 tsp salt

Instructions:

1. **Activate the Yeast:**
   - Dissolve molasses in warm water, sprinkle yeast over, and let sit for 5-10 minutes until frothy.
2. **Mix Dough:**
   - In a large bowl, combine rye flour, all-purpose flour, whole wheat flour, cocoa powder, caraway seeds (if using), and salt.
   - Add the yeast mixture and mix until a dough forms.
3. **Knead:**
   - Turn dough onto a floured surface and knead for about 8-10 minutes, until smooth.
4. **First Rise:**
   - Place dough in a greased bowl, cover, and let rise for 1-2 hours, or until doubled in size.
5. **Shape and Second Rise:**
   - Punch down the dough and shape it into a loaf.
   - Place in a greased loaf pan, cover, and let rise for 30-45 minutes.
6. **Bake:**
   - Preheat oven to 375°F (190°C).
   - Bake for 35-40 minutes, or until the bread is dark brown and sounds hollow when tapped.
7. **Cool:**
   - Let cool on a wire rack before slicing.

French Pain Complet

Ingredients:

- 3 cups whole wheat flour
- 1½ cups warm water
- 1 packet (2¼ tsp) active dry yeast
- 1 tbsp honey
- 1 tsp salt
- 2 tbsp olive oil

Instructions:

1. **Activate the Yeast:**
   - Dissolve honey in warm water, sprinkle yeast over, and let sit for 5-10 minutes until frothy.
2. **Mix Dough:**
   - In a large bowl, combine whole wheat flour and salt.
   - Add the yeast mixture and olive oil, and mix until a dough forms.
3. **Knead:**
   - Turn dough onto a floured surface and knead for about 8-10 minutes until smooth.
4. **First Rise:**
   - Place dough in a greased bowl, cover, and let rise for 1-2 hours, or until doubled in size.
5. **Shape and Second Rise:**
   - Punch down the dough and shape it into a loaf.
   - Place in a greased loaf pan, cover, and let rise for 30-45 minutes.
6. **Bake:**
   - Preheat oven to 375°F (190°C).
   - Bake for 30-35 minutes, or until the bread is brown and sounds hollow when tapped.
7. **Cool:**
   - Let cool on a wire rack before slicing.

Sweet Cornbread

Ingredients:

- 3 cups whole wheat flour
- 1½ cups warm water
- 1 packet (2¼ tsp) active dry yeast
- 1 tbsp honey
- 1 tsp salt
- 2 tbsp olive oil

Instructions:

1. **Activate the Yeast:**
   - Dissolve honey in warm water, sprinkle yeast over, and let sit for 5-10 minutes until frothy.
2. **Mix Dough:**
   - In a large bowl, combine whole wheat flour and salt.
   - Add the yeast mixture and olive oil, and mix until a dough forms.
3. **Knead:**
   - Turn dough onto a floured surface and knead for about 8-10 minutes until smooth.
4. **First Rise:**
   - Place dough in a greased bowl, cover, and let rise for 1-2 hours, or until doubled in size.
5. **Shape and Second Rise:**
   - Punch down the dough and shape it into a loaf.
   - Place in a greased loaf pan, cover, and let rise for 30-45 minutes.
6. **Bake:**
   - Preheat oven to 375°F (190°C).
   - Bake for 30-35 minutes, or until the bread is brown and sounds hollow when tapped.
7. **Cool:**
   - Let cool on a wire rack before slicing.

Sweet Cornbread

Ingredients:

- 1 cup cornmeal
- 1 cup all-purpose flour
- ¼ cup sugar
- 1 tbsp baking powder
- ½ tsp salt
- 1 cup milk
- 2 large eggs
- ¼ cup unsalted butter, melted
- 1 cup corn kernels (fresh, frozen, or canned, optional)

Instructions:

1. **Preheat Oven:**
   - Preheat your oven to 400°F (200°C). Grease an 8-inch square baking dish or a similarly sized oven-safe skillet.
2. **Mix Dry Ingredients:**
   - In a large bowl, whisk together cornmeal, flour, sugar, baking powder, and salt.
3. **Combine Wet Ingredients:**
   - In another bowl, beat the milk, eggs, and melted butter together.
4. **Mix the Batter:**
   - Pour the wet ingredients into the dry ingredients and stir until just combined.
   - If using corn kernels, fold them into the batter.
5. **Bake:**
   - Pour the batter into the prepared baking dish.
   - Bake for 20-25 minutes, or until the top is golden brown and a toothpick inserted into the center comes out clean.
6. **Cool:**
   - Let the cornbread cool in the pan for a few minutes before slicing and serving.

Enjoy your sweet cornbread warm, perhaps with a pat of butter or a drizzle of honey!

Tuscan Bread

Ingredients:

- 3 cups all-purpose flour
- 1 cup warm water
- 1 packet (2¼ tsp) active dry yeast
- 1 tsp salt
- 1 tbsp olive oil (optional, for extra flavor)

Instructions:

1. **Activate the Yeast:**
    - Dissolve yeast in warm water and let sit for 5-10 minutes until frothy.
2. **Mix the Dough:**
    - In a large bowl, combine flour and salt.
    - Add the yeast mixture (and olive oil, if using) and mix until a dough forms.
3. **Knead:**
    - Turn dough onto a floured surface and knead for about 10 minutes until smooth and elastic.
4. **First Rise:**
    - Place dough in a lightly oiled bowl, cover, and let rise for 1-2 hours, or until doubled in size.
5. **Shape and Second Rise:**
    - Punch down the dough and shape it into a round loaf.
    - Place on a parchment-lined baking sheet or in a greased round pan.
    - Cover and let rise for 30-45 minutes.
6. **Preheat Oven:**
    - Preheat oven to 450°F (230°C).
7. **Bake:**
    - Bake for 25-30 minutes, or until the bread is golden brown and sounds hollow when tapped.
8. **Cool:**
    - Let cool on a wire rack before slicing.

Enjoy your Tuscan bread with a drizzle of olive oil or alongside your favorite dishes!

Whole Wheat Sandwich Bread

Ingredients:

- 2 cups whole wheat flour
- 1 cup all-purpose flour
- 1½ cups warm water
- 1 packet (2¼ tsp) active dry yeast
- ¼ cup honey or maple syrup
- 2 tbsp olive oil
- 1½ tsp salt

Instructions:

1. **Activate the Yeast:**
   - Dissolve honey or maple syrup in warm water, sprinkle yeast over, and let sit for 5-10 minutes until frothy.
2. **Mix the Dough:**
   - In a large bowl, combine whole wheat flour, all-purpose flour, and salt.
   - Add the yeast mixture and olive oil. Stir until a dough forms.
3. **Knead:**
   - Turn dough onto a floured surface and knead for about 8-10 minutes, until smooth and elastic.
4. **First Rise:**
   - Place dough in a lightly oiled bowl, cover, and let rise for 1-1½ hours, or until doubled in size.
5. **Shape and Second Rise:**
   - Punch down the dough and shape it into a loaf.
   - Place in a greased 9x5-inch loaf pan.
   - Cover and let rise for 30-45 minutes, or until the dough has risen slightly above the rim of the pan.
6. **Preheat Oven:**
   - Preheat oven to 375°F (190°C).
7. **Bake:**
   - Bake for 30-35 minutes, or until the bread is golden brown and sounds hollow when tapped.
8. **Cool:**
   - Let the bread cool in the pan for 10 minutes, then transfer to a wire rack to cool completely before slicing.

This whole wheat sandwich bread is great for a variety of sandwiches and makes excellent toast!

Garlic Herb Bread

Ingredients:

- 3 cups all-purpose flour
- 1 cup warm water
- 1 packet (2¼ tsp) active dry yeast
- 2 tbsp olive oil
- 1 tsp sugar
- 1½ tsp salt
- 4 cloves garlic, minced
- 2 tbsp fresh parsley, chopped (or 2 tsp dried parsley)
- 1 tsp dried thyme
- 1 tsp dried rosemary

Instructions:

1. **Activate the Yeast:**
    - Dissolve sugar in warm water, sprinkle yeast over, and let sit for 5-10 minutes until frothy.
2. **Mix the Dough:**
    - In a large bowl, combine flour and salt.
    - Add the yeast mixture, olive oil, minced garlic, parsley, thyme, and rosemary.
    - Mix until a dough forms.
3. **Knead:**
    - Turn dough onto a floured surface and knead for about 8-10 minutes until smooth and elastic.
4. **First Rise:**
    - Place dough in a lightly oiled bowl, cover, and let rise for 1-1½ hours, or until doubled in size.
5. **Shape and Second Rise:**
    - Punch down the dough and shape it into a loaf.
    - Place in a greased 9x5-inch loaf pan.
    - Cover and let rise for 30-45 minutes, or until dough has risen slightly above the rim of the pan.
6. **Preheat Oven:**
    - Preheat oven to 375°F (190°C).
7. **Bake:**
    - Bake for 30-35 minutes, or until the bread is golden brown and sounds hollow when tapped.
8. **Cool:**
    - Let cool on a wire rack before slicing.

This Garlic Herb Bread is perfect for pairing with soups or enjoying with a bit of butter!

Scandinavian Crispbread

Ingredients:

- 1½ cups all-purpose flour
- 1½ cups whole wheat flour
- ½ cup rye flour (optional, for additional flavor)
- 1 tbsp sugar
- 1 tsp salt
- 2 tsp baking powder
- ¼ cup vegetable oil or melted butter
- 1 cup water
- 2 tbsp caraway seeds or sesame seeds (optional, for topping)

Instructions:

1. **Preheat Oven:**
   - Preheat your oven to 400°F (200°C).
2. **Mix Dry Ingredients:**
   - In a large bowl, whisk together all-purpose flour, whole wheat flour, rye flour (if using), sugar, salt, and baking powder.
3. **Combine Wet Ingredients:**
   - Add the vegetable oil or melted butter to the dry ingredients.
   - Gradually add water, mixing until a dough forms.
4. **Roll Out Dough:**
   - Turn the dough onto a floured surface and roll it out as thin as possible, about 1/8-inch thick.
5. **Cut and Puncture:**
   - Cut the dough into squares or rectangles using a knife or pizza cutter.
   - Puncture the dough with a fork to prevent puffing during baking.
6. **Add Toppings:**
   - If desired, sprinkle the tops with caraway seeds or sesame seeds for extra flavor and texture.
7. **Bake:**
   - Place the cut dough on a baking sheet lined with parchment paper.
   - Bake for 10-15 minutes, or until crisp and golden brown. The crispbread should be crunchy and dry.
8. **Cool:**
   - Let the crispbread cool on a wire rack before storing.

Scandinavian Crispbread is perfect for snacking or as an accompaniment to cheese, spreads, or soups. Enjoy its delightful crunch and versatility!

Cinnamon Raisin Bread

Ingredients:

- 3½ cups all-purpose flour
- 1 packet (2¼ tsp) active dry yeast
- 1 cup milk
- ¼ cup sugar
- ¼ cup unsalted butter, softened
- 1 tsp salt
- 1 large egg
- 1 cup raisins
- 2 tbsp ground cinnamon
- ¼ cup brown sugar

Instructions:

1. **Prepare the Dough:**
    - Warm the milk to about 110°F (45°C). Dissolve ¼ cup sugar in the milk, then sprinkle the yeast over and let sit for 5-10 minutes until frothy.
2. **Mix the Dough:**
    - In a large bowl, combine flour and salt.
    - Add the yeast mixture, softened butter, and egg. Mix until a dough forms.
3. **Knead:**
    - Turn the dough onto a floured surface and knead for about 8-10 minutes until smooth.
4. **Add Raisins:**
    - Flatten the dough slightly and sprinkle raisins evenly over it. Fold the dough to distribute the raisins, then knead a few more minutes.
5. **First Rise:**
    - Place dough in a lightly oiled bowl, cover, and let rise for 1-1½ hours, or until doubled.
6. **Shape and Second Rise:**
    - Punch down the dough and shape it into a loaf.
    - Place in a greased 9x5-inch loaf pan.
    - Cover and let rise for 30-45 minutes.
7. **Prepare Cinnamon Sugar:**
    - In a small bowl, mix ¼ cup brown sugar with 2 tbsp ground cinnamon.
8. **Bake:**
    - Preheat oven to 350°F (175°C).
    - Before baking, sprinkle the cinnamon sugar mixture on top of the loaf.

- Bake for 35-40 minutes, or until golden brown and a toothpick inserted into the center comes out clean.
9. **Cool:**
    - Let cool on a wire rack before slicing.

Enjoy this sweet and aromatic Cinnamon Raisin Bread as a treat for breakfast or a snack!

Pane Carasau

Ingredients:

- 3 cups all-purpose flour
- 1 cup warm water
- 1 packet (2¼ tsp) active dry yeast
- 1 tsp salt
- 1 tbsp olive oil

Instructions:

1. **Activate the Yeast:**
    - Dissolve yeast in warm water and let sit for 5-10 minutes until frothy.
2. **Mix the Dough:**
    - In a large bowl, combine flour and salt.
    - Add the yeast mixture and olive oil. Mix until a dough forms.
3. **Knead:**
    - Turn dough onto a floured surface and knead for about 8-10 minutes until smooth and elastic.
4. **First Rise:**
    - Place dough in a lightly oiled bowl, cover, and let rise for 1-2 hours, or until doubled.
5. **Shape and Roll:**
    - Punch down dough and divide into 4-6 pieces.
    - Roll each piece into a thin, round sheet about 1/8 inch thick.
6. **Bake:**
    - Preheat oven to 450°F (230°C).
    - Place dough on a baking sheet and bake for 3-5 minutes until lightly golden and puffed.
    - Remove from oven and let cool slightly, then split each piece in half to create the crisp layers.
7. **Cool:**
    - Let the Pane Carasau cool completely before serving. It should be crisp and crackly.

Pane Carasau is perfect as a snack or accompaniment to soups and salads. Enjoy its unique, crunchy texture!

Stuffed Focaccia

Ingredients:

Dough:

- 3½ cups all-purpose flour
- 1 packet (2¼ tsp) active dry yeast
- 1½ cups warm water
- ¼ cup olive oil, plus extra for drizzling
- 1 tbsp sugar
- 1½ tsp salt

Filling:

- 1 cup shredded mozzarella cheese
- ½ cup grated Parmesan cheese
- 1 cup cooked spinach, squeezed dry and chopped (or other filling like sun-dried tomatoes, olives, or caramelized onions)
- 2-3 cloves garlic, minced
- 1 tsp dried oregano
- Fresh rosemary (optional)

Instructions:

1. **Prepare the Dough:**
   - Dissolve sugar in warm water, sprinkle yeast over, and let sit for 5-10 minutes until frothy.
   - In a large bowl, combine flour and salt.
   - Add the yeast mixture and olive oil. Mix until a dough forms.
2. **Knead:**
   - Turn dough onto a floured surface and knead for about 8-10 minutes until smooth and elastic.
3. **First Rise:**
   - Place dough in a lightly oiled bowl, cover, and let rise for 1-1½ hours, or until doubled in size.
4. **Prepare Filling:**
   - Mix together the mozzarella, Parmesan, spinach (or other fillings), minced garlic, and oregano in a bowl.
5. **Shape and Stuff:**
   - Punch down the dough and divide it in half.
   - Roll out the first half into a rectangle and place it on a greased baking sheet.

- Spread the filling evenly over the dough, then cover with the second rolled-out half of dough. Pinch the edges to seal.
6. **Second Rise:**
    - Cover and let rise for 30 minutes.
7. **Preheat Oven:**
    - Preheat oven to 425°F (220°C).
8. **Bake:**
    - Drizzle the top with olive oil and sprinkle with fresh rosemary if desired.
    - Bake for 25-30 minutes, or until golden brown and crispy on top.
9. **Cool:**
    - Let cool slightly before slicing and serving.

This Stuffed Focaccia is perfect as an appetizer or a hearty side dish!

Naan

Ingredients:

- 2¼ tsp active dry yeast (1 packet)
- 1 cup warm milk
- 2 tbsp sugar
- 3½ cups all-purpose flour
- 1 tsp salt
- ¼ cup plain yogurt
- 2 tbsp olive oil or melted butter
- 1 large egg (optional, for extra softness)
- 3-4 cloves garlic, minced (optional, for garlic naan)

Instructions:

1. **Activate the Yeast:**
   - Dissolve sugar in warm milk, then sprinkle yeast over. Let sit for 5-10 minutes until frothy.
2. **Mix the Dough:**
   - In a large bowl, combine flour and salt.
   - Add the yeast mixture, yogurt, and olive oil. Mix until a dough forms. If using, add the egg.
3. **Knead:**
   - Turn dough onto a floured surface and knead for about 8 minutes until smooth and elastic.
4. **First Rise:**
   - Place dough in a lightly oiled bowl, cover, and let rise for 1-2 hours, or until doubled in size.
5. **Shape the Naan:**
   - Punch down the dough and divide into 8-10 pieces.
   - Roll each piece into a tear-shaped or round flatbread about ¼ inch thick.
6. **Cook:**
   - Preheat a cast-iron skillet or heavy-bottomed pan over medium-high heat.
   - Place the naan in the skillet and cook for 1-2 minutes, until bubbles form. Flip and cook for another 1-2 minutes, or until lightly browned.
   - For garlic naan, brush with melted butter and sprinkle minced garlic before cooking.
7. **Serve:**
   - Brush with more melted butter if desired. Serve warm.

Enjoy your homemade naan with curry, or as a delicious accompaniment to any meal!

Pretzel Rolls

Ingredients:

- 2¼ tsp active dry yeast (1 packet)
- 1¼ cups warm water
- 1 tbsp sugar
- 3½ cups all-purpose flour
- 1 tsp salt
- 2 tbsp unsalted butter, melted
- ¼ cup baking soda
- 1 large egg, beaten (for egg wash)
- Coarse sea salt (for topping)

Instructions:

1. **Activate the Yeast:**
   - Dissolve sugar in warm water, sprinkle yeast over, and let sit for 5-10 minutes until frothy.
2. **Mix the Dough:**
   - In a large bowl, combine flour and salt.
   - Add the yeast mixture and melted butter. Mix until a dough forms.
3. **Knead:**
   - Turn dough onto a floured surface and knead for about 8 minutes until smooth and elastic.
4. **First Rise:**
   - Place dough in a lightly oiled bowl, cover, and let rise for 1-1½ hours, or until doubled.
5. **Shape and Second Rise:**
   - Punch down the dough and divide into 12-15 pieces. Shape each piece into a ball and place on a parchment-lined baking sheet.
   - Cover and let rise for 30 minutes.
6. **Prepare Baking Soda Solution:**
   - Preheat oven to 400°F (200°C).
   - In a large pot, bring 6 cups of water and baking soda to a boil.
7. **Boil the Rolls:**
   - Drop rolls into the boiling water, 2-3 at a time, and boil for about 30 seconds, flipping halfway through.
   - Remove with a slotted spoon and place back on the baking sheet.
8. **Apply Egg Wash:**
   - Brush each roll with the beaten egg and sprinkle with coarse sea salt.
9. **Bake:**

- Bake for 15-20 minutes, or until golden brown.
10. **Cool:**
    - Let cool slightly before serving.

These Pretzel Rolls are perfect for sandwiches or as a tasty snack on their own!

Dutch Oven Bread

Ingredients:

- 3 cups all-purpose flour
- 1¼ tsp salt
- ½ tsp instant yeast
- 1¼ cups warm water (about 110°F or 45°C)

Instructions:

1. **Mix the Dough:**
   - In a large bowl, whisk together the flour, salt, and yeast.
   - Add the warm water and stir until a shaggy dough forms.
2. **First Rise:**
   - Cover the bowl with plastic wrap or a damp cloth.
   - Let the dough rise at room temperature for 12-18 hours. The dough should be bubbly and doubled in size.
3. **Shape the Dough:**
   - Lightly flour a work surface and turn the dough out onto it.
   - Gently shape the dough into a round loaf, being careful not to deflate it too much.
4. **Preheat the Dutch Oven:**
   - Place your Dutch oven (with the lid on) in the oven.
   - Preheat the oven to 450°F (230°C) and let the Dutch oven heat up for about 30 minutes.
5. **Prepare for Baking:**
   - Carefully remove the hot Dutch oven from the oven.
   - Place the dough into the Dutch oven. If desired, you can score the top of the loaf with a sharp knife or a bread lame.
6. **Bake:**
   - Cover the Dutch oven with its lid and bake for 30 minutes.
   - After 30 minutes, remove the lid and bake for an additional 15-20 minutes, or until the bread is deep golden brown and sounds hollow when tapped.
7. **Cool:**
   - Remove the bread from the Dutch oven and let it cool on a wire rack before slicing.

Enjoy your Dutch Oven Bread with butter, cheese, or your favorite spread! The crispy crust and chewy interior make it perfect for a variety of uses.

Soda Bread with Caraway

Ingredients:

- 4 cups all-purpose flour
- 1 tsp baking soda
- 1 tsp salt
- 2 tbsp caraway seeds
- 1½ cups buttermilk (or 1½ cups milk plus 1½ tbsp lemon juice or white vinegar)

Instructions:

1. **Preheat Oven:**
   - Preheat your oven to 425°F (220°C).
   - Grease a 9-inch round baking pan or line it with parchment paper.
2. **Mix Dry Ingredients:**
   - In a large bowl, whisk together flour, baking soda, salt, and caraway seeds.
3. **Add Buttermilk:**
   - Make a well in the center of the dry ingredients and pour in the buttermilk.
   - Stir with a wooden spoon or your hands until a sticky dough forms. Do not overmix; the dough should be just combined.
4. **Shape the Dough:**
   - Turn the dough out onto a lightly floured surface and shape it into a round loaf.
   - Place the loaf in the prepared baking pan.
5. **Score the Dough:**
   - Using a sharp knife, cut a deep cross into the top of the dough. This helps the bread cook evenly and gives it a classic soda bread appearance.
6. **Bake:**
   - Bake in the preheated oven for 35-45 minutes, or until the bread is golden brown and sounds hollow when tapped on the bottom.
7. **Cool:**
   - Let the bread cool on a wire rack before slicing.

Enjoy your Soda Bread with Caraway Seeds warm with butter, or as a side to your favorite soups and stews!

Rye with Seeds

Ingredients:

- 1½ cups rye flour
- 1½ cups all-purpose flour
- 1 packet (2¼ tsp) active dry yeast
- 1½ cups warm water
- 2 tbsp honey
- 1 tbsp caraway seeds
- 1 tbsp sunflower seeds
- 1 tbsp sesame seeds
- 1 tsp salt
- 1 tbsp vegetable oil

Instructions:

1. **Activate the Yeast:**
   - Dissolve honey in warm water, sprinkle yeast over, and let sit for 5-10 minutes until frothy.
2. **Mix the Dough:**
   - In a large bowl, combine rye flour, all-purpose flour, and salt.
   - Add the yeast mixture and vegetable oil. Mix until a dough forms.
3. **Add Seeds:**
   - Stir in caraway seeds, sunflower seeds, and sesame seeds.
4. **Knead:**
   - Turn dough onto a floured surface and knead for about 8-10 minutes until smooth and elastic.
5. **First Rise:**
   - Place dough in a lightly oiled bowl, cover, and let rise for 1-1½ hours, or until doubled in size.
6. **Shape and Second Rise:**
   - Punch down the dough and shape it into a loaf.
   - Place in a greased 9x5-inch loaf pan.
   - Cover and let rise for 30-45 minutes.
7. **Preheat Oven:**
   - Preheat oven to 375°F (190°C).
8. **Bake:**
   - Bake for 35-40 minutes, or until the bread is golden brown and sounds hollow when tapped.
9. **Cool:**
   - Let cool on a wire rack before slicing.

This Rye Bread with Seeds offers a hearty texture and rich flavor, perfect for sandwiches or served with soups and stews.

Coconut Bread

Ingredients:

- 2 cups all-purpose flour
- 1 cup sweetened shredded coconut
- 1 cup granulated sugar
- 1 tbsp baking powder
- ½ tsp salt
- ½ cup unsalted butter, melted
- 1 cup milk
- 2 large eggs
- 1 tsp vanilla extract

Instructions:

1. **Preheat Oven:**
    - Preheat your oven to 350°F (175°C).
    - Grease a 9x5-inch loaf pan or line it with parchment paper.
2. **Mix Dry Ingredients:**
    - In a large bowl, whisk together flour, sugar, shredded coconut, baking powder, and salt.
3. **Combine Wet Ingredients:**
    - In another bowl, whisk together melted butter, milk, eggs, and vanilla extract.
4. **Mix the Batter:**
    - Pour the wet ingredients into the dry ingredients and stir until just combined. Do not overmix.
5. **Bake:**
    - Pour the batter into the prepared loaf pan.
    - Bake for 50-60 minutes, or until a toothpick inserted into the center comes out clean and the top is golden brown.
6. **Cool:**
    - Let the bread cool in the pan for 10 minutes, then transfer to a wire rack to cool completely before slicing.

This Coconut Bread is wonderfully moist and lightly sweet, perfect for breakfast or as a snack!

Black Bread

Ingredients:

- 2 cups rye flour
- 1 cup all-purpose flour
- 1 packet (2¼ tsp) active dry yeast
- 1½ cups warm water
- 2 tbsp molasses or dark brown sugar
- 1 tbsp caraway seeds (optional)
- 1 tbsp cocoa powder
- 1 tsp salt
- 2 tbsp vegetable oil or melted butter

Instructions:

1. **Activate the Yeast:**
   - Dissolve molasses or sugar in warm water, sprinkle yeast over, and let sit for 5-10 minutes until frothy.
2. **Mix the Dough:**
   - In a large bowl, combine rye flour, all-purpose flour, cocoa powder, and salt.
   - Add the yeast mixture and vegetable oil. Mix until a dough forms. If using caraway seeds, stir them into the dough.
3. **Knead:**
   - Turn dough onto a floured surface and knead for about 8-10 minutes until smooth and elastic. The dough will be somewhat sticky due to the rye flour.
4. **First Rise:**
   - Place dough in a lightly oiled bowl, cover, and let rise for 1-1½ hours, or until doubled in size.
5. **Shape and Second Rise:**
   - Punch down the dough and shape it into a loaf. You can also shape it into a round if preferred.
   - Place the loaf in a greased 9x5-inch loaf pan or on a baking sheet.
   - Cover and let rise for 30-45 minutes.
6. **Preheat Oven:**
   - Preheat oven to 375°F (190°C).
7. **Bake:**
   - Bake for 35-40 minutes, or until the bread is dark brown and sounds hollow when tapped on the bottom. The internal temperature should be around 190°F (88°C).
8. **Cool:**
   - Let the bread cool on a wire rack before slicing.

This Black Bread is rich and hearty, with a deep flavor from the rye flour and cocoa powder. It's excellent with cheese, cold cuts, or as a base for robust sandwiches.

Oatmeal Bread

Ingredients:

- 1 cup old-fashioned rolled oats
- 1¼ cups warm water (110°F or 45°C)
- 1 packet (2¼ tsp) active dry yeast
- 2 tbsp honey or maple syrup
- 2 tbsp unsalted butter, softened
- 2½ cups all-purpose flour
- 1 tsp salt

Instructions:

1. **Prepare the Oats:**
    - In a bowl, combine the rolled oats with 1¼ cups of warm water. Let sit for 10-15 minutes to soften.
2. **Activate the Yeast:**
    - In a small bowl, dissolve honey or maple syrup in ¼ cup of warm water. Sprinkle the yeast over and let sit for 5-10 minutes until frothy.
3. **Mix the Dough:**
    - In a large bowl, combine flour and salt.
    - Add the softened oats (including any water they soaked in), the yeast mixture, and the softened butter. Mix until a dough forms.
4. **Knead:**
    - Turn the dough onto a floured surface and knead for about 8-10 minutes until smooth and elastic.
5. **First Rise:**
    - Place dough in a lightly oiled bowl, cover, and let rise for 1-1½ hours, or until doubled in size.
6. **Shape and Second Rise:**
    - Punch down the dough and shape it into a loaf.
    - Place it in a greased 9x5-inch loaf pan.
    - Cover and let rise for 30-45 minutes, or until the dough has risen slightly above the rim of the pan.
7. **Preheat Oven:**
    - Preheat oven to 375°F (190°C).
8. **Bake:**
    - Bake for 30-35 minutes, or until the bread is golden brown and sounds hollow when tapped on the bottom.
9. **Cool:**

- Let the bread cool in the pan for 10 minutes, then transfer to a wire rack to cool completely before slicing.

This Oatmeal Bread is soft and slightly nutty, perfect for sandwiches, toast, or just enjoying with a bit of butter.

Cheese Bread

Ingredients:

- 2 cups all-purpose flour
- 1 tbsp baking powder
- ½ tsp salt
- 1 cup shredded cheese (cheddar, mozzarella, or your choice)
- 1 cup milk
- ¼ cup vegetable oil or melted butter
- 2 large eggs

Instructions:

1. **Preheat Oven:**
   - Preheat your oven to 375°F (190°C).
   - Grease a 9x5-inch loaf pan or line it with parchment paper.
2. **Mix Dry Ingredients:**
   - In a large bowl, whisk together flour, baking powder, and salt.
3. **Add Cheese:**
   - Stir in the shredded cheese until evenly distributed.
4. **Combine Wet Ingredients:**
   - In another bowl, whisk together milk, vegetable oil (or melted butter), and eggs.
5. **Mix the Batter:**
   - Pour the wet ingredients into the dry ingredients and stir until just combined. Be careful not to overmix.
6. **Bake:**
   - Pour the batter into the prepared loaf pan.
   - Bake for 35-40 minutes, or until the top is golden brown and a toothpick inserted into the center comes out clean.
7. **Cool:**
   - Let the bread cool in the pan for 10 minutes before transferring it to a wire rack to cool completely.

This Cheese Bread is great warm or at room temperature, and it's perfect as a snack, side dish, or for making sandwiches. Enjoy the cheesy goodness!

Baghrir (Moroccan Pancake Bread)

Ingredients:

- 1 cup semolina
- ½ cup all-purpose flour
- 1 tsp active dry yeast
- 1 tsp baking powder
- ½ tsp salt
- 1½ cups warm water
- 1 tbsp honey or sugar (optional, for a touch of sweetness)

Instructions:

1. **Prepare the Batter:**
    - In a large bowl, combine semolina, flour, yeast, baking powder, and salt.
    - Gradually add warm water and honey (if using), whisking until smooth.
2. **Let the Batter Rise:**
    - Cover the bowl with plastic wrap or a damp cloth.
    - Let the batter rest in a warm place for 1-2 hours, or until bubbles form on the surface and it becomes slightly foamy.
3. **Preheat Pan:**
    - Heat a non-stick skillet or crepe pan over medium heat. No need to grease the pan.
4. **Cook the Baghrir:**
    - Pour about ¼ cup of batter onto the pan and spread it into a round shape.
    - Cook until bubbles form on the surface and the edges look set, about 2-3 minutes. The bottom should be lightly golden.
    - Do not flip; cook only on one side.
5. **Serve:**
    - Serve warm with honey, butter, or jam. Baghrir is also great with a drizzle of olive oil or sprinkled with sesame seeds.

Enjoy these fluffy, spongy Moroccan pancakes with your favorite toppings!

Pain d'épi

Ingredients:

- 3½ cups all-purpose flour
- 1 packet (2¼ tsp) active dry yeast
- 1½ cups warm water (110°F or 45°C)
- 1 tbsp sugar
- 1½ tsp salt
- 2 tbsp olive oil

Instructions:

1. **Activate the Yeast:**
    - Dissolve sugar in warm water. Sprinkle the yeast over the water and let sit for 5-10 minutes until frothy.
2. **Mix the Dough:**
    - In a large bowl, combine flour and salt.
    - Add the yeast mixture and olive oil. Mix until a dough forms.
3. **Knead:**
    - Turn the dough onto a floured surface and knead for about 8-10 minutes until smooth and elastic.
4. **First Rise:**
    - Place dough in a lightly oiled bowl, cover, and let rise for 1-1½ hours, or until doubled in size.
5. **Shape the Dough:**
    - Punch down the dough and shape it into a round loaf.
    - Transfer the loaf to a baking sheet lined with parchment paper.
6. **Shape into Épi:**
    - Using a sharp knife or dough cutter, score the dough to create a pattern resembling a stalk of wheat. To do this, make long cuts radiating from the center to the edges of the loaf, slightly angling the cuts to mimic the look of grain stalks.
7. **Second Rise:**
    - Cover the loaf and let it rise for another 30-45 minutes, or until it has risen slightly.
8. **Preheat Oven:**
    - Preheat oven to 375°F (190°C).
9. **Bake:**
    - Bake for 25-35 minutes, or until the bread is golden brown and sounds hollow when tapped on the bottom.
10. **Cool:**
    - Let the bread cool on a wire rack before slicing.

Pain d'Épi is not only delicious but also visually striking, making it a perfect centerpiece for special occasions or festive meals. Enjoy the beautiful and flavorful bread!

Semolina Bread

Ingredients:

- 2 cups semolina flour
- 1 cup all-purpose flour
- 1 packet (2¼ tsp) active dry yeast
- 1¼ cups warm water (110°F or 45°C)
- 1 tbsp honey or sugar
- 1½ tsp salt
- 2 tbsp olive oil

Instructions:

1. **Activate the Yeast:**
    - Dissolve honey or sugar in warm water. Sprinkle the yeast over the water and let sit for 5-10 minutes until frothy.
2. **Mix the Dough:**
    - In a large bowl, combine semolina flour, all-purpose flour, and salt.
    - Add the yeast mixture and olive oil. Mix until a dough forms.
3. **Knead:**
    - Turn the dough onto a floured surface and knead for about 8-10 minutes until smooth and elastic.
4. **First Rise:**
    - Place dough in a lightly oiled bowl, cover, and let rise for 1-1½ hours, or until doubled in size.
5. **Shape and Second Rise:**
    - Punch down the dough and shape it into a loaf. Alternatively, you can shape it into a round or bâtard shape.
    - Place the loaf in a greased 9x5-inch loaf pan or on a baking sheet.
    - Cover and let rise for 30-45 minutes, or until it has risen slightly above the rim of the pan.
6. **Preheat Oven:**
    - Preheat your oven to 375°F (190°C).
7. **Bake:**
    - Bake for 30-35 minutes, or until the bread is golden brown and sounds hollow when tapped on the bottom.
8. **Cool:**
    - Let the bread cool on a wire rack before slicing.

This Semolina Bread has a wonderful texture and flavor, perfect for sandwiches or simply toasted with butter. Enjoy!

Spelt Bread

Ingredients:

- 3 cups spelt flour
- 1 cup all-purpose flour (optional, for a lighter texture; you can use all spelt flour if preferred)
- 1 packet (2¼ tsp) active dry yeast
- 1½ cups warm water (110°F or 45°C)
- 2 tbsp honey or maple syrup
- 1½ tsp salt
- 2 tbsp olive oil or melted butter

Instructions:

1. **Activate the Yeast:**
   - Dissolve honey or maple syrup in warm water. Sprinkle the yeast over the water and let sit for 5-10 minutes until frothy.
2. **Mix the Dough:**
   - In a large bowl, combine spelt flour, all-purpose flour (if using), and salt.
   - Add the yeast mixture and olive oil (or melted butter). Mix until a dough forms.
3. **Knead:**
   - Turn the dough onto a floured surface and knead for about 8-10 minutes until smooth and elastic. The dough may be slightly sticky; this is normal with spelt flour.
4. **First Rise:**
   - Place dough in a lightly oiled bowl, cover, and let rise for 1-1½ hours, or until doubled in size.
5. **Shape and Second Rise:**
   - Punch down the dough and shape it into a loaf. Place it in a greased 9x5-inch loaf pan or shape it into a round loaf and place it on a baking sheet.
   - Cover and let rise for 30-45 minutes, or until it has risen slightly above the rim of the pan.
6. **Preheat Oven:**
   - Preheat your oven to 375°F (190°C).
7. **Bake:**
   - Bake for 30-35 minutes, or until the bread is golden brown and sounds hollow when tapped on the bottom.
8. **Cool:**
   - Let the bread cool on a wire rack before slicing.

Spelt Bread is great for sandwiches, toast, or simply enjoyed with a bit of butter. Its nutty flavor and slightly dense texture make it a nutritious and delicious choice!

Soft Pretzel Bites

Ingredients:

For the Pretzel Bites:

- 1½ cups warm water (110°F or 45°C)
- 1 packet (2¼ tsp) active dry yeast
- 1 tbsp granulated sugar
- 4 cups all-purpose flour
- 1 tsp salt
- 2 tbsp unsalted butter, melted

For the Baking Soda Bath:

- 10 cups water
- ⅔ cup baking soda

For Topping:

- Coarse sea salt
- 2 tbsp melted butter (for brushing)

Instructions:

1. **Activate the Yeast:**
   - In a large bowl, combine warm water and sugar. Sprinkle yeast over the top and let sit for 5-10 minutes, until frothy.
2. **Mix the Dough:**
   - Add flour and salt to the yeast mixture. Mix until combined, then add melted butter. Knead the dough for about 8 minutes until smooth and elastic.
3. **First Rise:**
   - Place dough in a lightly oiled bowl, cover, and let rise in a warm place for 1 hour, or until doubled in size.
4. **Prepare the Baking Soda Bath:**
   - In a large pot, bring water and baking soda to a boil.
5. **Shape the Pretzel Bites:**
   - Punch down the dough and turn it onto a floured surface. Divide the dough into small pieces, about 1-inch each.
   - Roll each piece into a small ball.
6. **Boil the Pretzel Bites:**
   - Drop the pretzel bites into the boiling baking soda bath, a few at a time, for 30 seconds. Use a slotted spoon to remove them and place them on a parchment-lined baking sheet.
7. **Add Topping:**
   - Brush the pretzel bites with melted butter and sprinkle with coarse sea salt.
8. **Bake:**

- Preheat your oven to 425°F (220°C).
- Bake for 10-12 minutes, or until the pretzel bites are golden brown.

9. **Cool:**
    - Let cool slightly before serving. They are best enjoyed warm.

Serve these Soft Pretzel Bites with your favorite dipping sauces, such as mustard, cheese sauce, or a spicy dipping sauce. Enjoy!

Kamut Bread

Ingredients:

- 2 cups Kamut flour
- 1 cup all-purpose flour (optional, for lighter texture; you can use all Kamut flour if preferred)
- 1 packet (2¼ tsp) active dry yeast
- 1½ cups warm water (110°F or 45°C)
- 2 tbsp honey or maple syrup
- 1½ tsp salt
- 2 tbsp olive oil or melted butter

Instructions:

1. **Activate the Yeast:**
   - Dissolve honey or maple syrup in warm water. Sprinkle the yeast over and let sit for 5-10 minutes until frothy.
2. **Mix the Dough:**
   - In a large bowl, combine Kamut flour, all-purpose flour (if using), and salt.
   - Add the yeast mixture and olive oil (or melted butter). Mix until a dough forms.
3. **Knead:**
   - Turn the dough onto a floured surface and knead for about 8-10 minutes until smooth and elastic. Kamut flour can be slightly coarse, so the dough might be a bit denser.
4. **First Rise:**
   - Place the dough in a lightly oiled bowl, cover, and let rise for 1-1½ hours, or until doubled in size.
5. **Shape and Second Rise:**
   - Punch down the dough and shape it into a loaf. Place it in a greased 9x5-inch loaf pan or shape it into a round loaf and place it on a baking sheet.
   - Cover and let rise for 30-45 minutes, or until it has risen slightly above the rim of the pan.
6. **Preheat Oven:**
   - Preheat your oven to 375°F (190°C).
7. **Bake:**
   - Bake for 30-35 minutes, or until the bread is golden brown and sounds hollow when tapped on the bottom.
8. **Cool:**
   - Let the bread cool on a wire rack before slicing.

Kamut Bread has a rich, nutty flavor and is perfect for sandwiches or served with soups and stews. Enjoy the unique taste of Kamut!

Kumara (Sweet Potato) Bread

Ingredients:

- 1 cup cooked and mashed sweet potato (about 1 medium sweet potato)
- 3 cups all-purpose flour
- ¼ cup brown sugar
- 1 packet (2¼ tsp) active dry yeast
- 1½ cups warm water (110°F or 45°C)
- 1½ tsp salt
- 2 tbsp unsalted butter, melted
- 1 tsp ground cinnamon (optional, for added flavor)

Instructions:

1. **Prepare the Sweet Potato:**
    - Cook the sweet potato until tender. You can bake, boil, or microwave it. Peel and mash until smooth. Measure out 1 cup.
2. **Activate the Yeast:**
    - In a small bowl, dissolve ¼ cup of the brown sugar in warm water. Sprinkle the yeast over and let sit for 5-10 minutes until frothy.
3. **Mix the Dough:**
    - In a large bowl, combine flour, salt, and cinnamon (if using).
    - Add the yeast mixture, mashed sweet potato, and melted butter. Mix until a dough forms.
4. **Knead:**
    - Turn the dough onto a floured surface and knead for about 8-10 minutes until smooth and elastic. The dough should be slightly sticky but manageable.
5. **First Rise:**
    - Place the dough in a lightly oiled bowl, cover, and let rise in a warm place for 1-1½ hours, or until doubled in size.
6. **Shape and Second Rise:**
    - Punch down the dough and shape it into a loaf. Place it in a greased 9x5-inch loaf pan or shape it into a round loaf and place it on a baking sheet.
    - Cover and let rise for 30-45 minutes, or until it has risen slightly above the rim of the pan.
7. **Preheat Oven:**
    - Preheat your oven to 375°F (190°C).
8. **Bake:**
    - Bake for 35-40 minutes, or until the bread is golden brown and sounds hollow when tapped on the bottom.
9. **Cool:**

- Let the bread cool on a wire rack before slicing.

Kumara Bread is sweet and tender, making it perfect for breakfast or as a snack. It pairs wonderfully with butter, cream cheese, or simply enjoyed on its own. Enjoy your delicious, sweet potato bread!

Sesame Seed Bread

Ingredients:

- 3 cups all-purpose flour
- 1 packet (2¼ tsp) active dry yeast
- 1½ cups warm water (110°F or 45°C)
- 2 tbsp honey or sugar
- 1½ tsp salt
- 2 tbsp olive oil or melted butter
- ¼ cup sesame seeds (for topping)
- 2 tbsp sesame seeds (for mixing into the dough)

Instructions:

1. **Activate the Yeast:**
   - Dissolve honey or sugar in warm water. Sprinkle yeast over and let sit for 5-10 minutes until frothy.
2. **Mix the Dough:**
   - In a large bowl, combine flour, salt, and 2 tbsp sesame seeds.
   - Add the yeast mixture and olive oil (or melted butter). Mix until a dough forms.
3. **Knead:**
   - Turn the dough onto a floured surface and knead for about 8-10 minutes until smooth and elastic.
4. **First Rise:**
   - Place the dough in a lightly oiled bowl, cover, and let rise for 1-1½ hours, or until doubled in size.
5. **Shape and Second Rise:**
   - Punch down the dough and shape it into a loaf.
   - Place it in a greased 9x5-inch loaf pan or shape it into a round loaf and place it on a baking sheet.
   - Cover and let rise for 30-45 minutes, or until slightly above the rim of the pan.
6. **Preheat Oven:**
   - Preheat your oven to 375°F (190°C).
7. **Prepare for Baking:**
   - Brush the top of the loaf with a little water or melted butter and sprinkle with ¼ cup sesame seeds.
8. **Bake:**
   - Bake for 30-35 minutes, or until the bread is golden brown and sounds hollow when tapped on the bottom.
9. **Cool:**
   - Let the bread cool on a wire rack before slicing.

Sesame Seed Bread has a wonderful texture and nutty flavor, perfect for sandwiches, toasts, or simply enjoyed with a bit of butter. Enjoy your freshly baked bread!

Olive Oil Bread

Ingredients:

- 3 cups all-purpose flour
- 1 packet (2¼ tsp) active dry yeast
- 1½ cups warm water (110°F or 45°C)
- ¼ cup extra virgin olive oil
- 1 tbsp honey or sugar
- 1½ tsp salt

Instructions:

1. **Activate the Yeast:**
   - Dissolve honey or sugar in warm water. Sprinkle yeast over and let sit for 5-10 minutes until frothy.
2. **Mix the Dough:**
   - In a large bowl, combine flour and salt.
   - Add the yeast mixture and olive oil. Mix until a dough forms.
3. **Knead:**
   - Turn the dough onto a floured surface and knead for about 8-10 minutes until smooth and elastic.
4. **First Rise:**
   - Place dough in a lightly oiled bowl, cover, and let rise in a warm place for 1-1½ hours, or until doubled in size.
5. **Shape and Second Rise:**
   - Punch down the dough and shape it into a loaf or divide it into smaller loaves.
   - Place the loaf in a greased 9x5-inch loaf pan or on a baking sheet.
   - Cover and let rise for 30-45 minutes, or until slightly above the rim of the pan.
6. **Preheat Oven:**
   - Preheat your oven to 375°F (190°C).
7. **Bake:**
   - Bake for 25-30 minutes, or until the bread is golden brown and sounds hollow when tapped on the bottom.
8. **Cool:**
   - Let the bread cool on a wire rack before slicing.

Olive Oil Bread has a delightful texture and flavor, making it perfect for dipping in soups, enjoying with cheese, or as a side with any meal. Enjoy the rich taste of olive oil in every bite!

Pane Siciliano

Ingredients:

- 3 cups all-purpose flour
- 1 cup semolina flour
- 1 packet (2¼ tsp) active dry yeast
- 1½ cups warm water (110°F or 45°C)
- 2 tbsp olive oil
- 1 tbsp honey or sugar
- 1½ tsp salt
- 1 tbsp sesame seeds (optional, for topping)

Instructions:

1. **Activate the Yeast:**
   - Dissolve honey or sugar in warm water. Sprinkle the yeast over and let sit for 5-10 minutes until frothy.
2. **Mix the Dough:**
   - In a large bowl, combine all-purpose flour, semolina flour, and salt.
   - Add the yeast mixture and olive oil. Mix until a dough forms.
3. **Knead:**
   - Turn the dough onto a floured surface and knead for about 8-10 minutes until smooth and elastic.
4. **First Rise:**
   - Place the dough in a lightly oiled bowl, cover, and let rise in a warm place for 1-1½ hours, or until doubled in size.
5. **Shape and Second Rise:**
   - Punch down the dough and shape it into a round or oval loaf.
   - Place the loaf on a parchment-lined baking sheet or a floured baking surface.
   - Cover and let rise for 30-45 minutes, or until slightly above the rim.
6. **Preheat Oven:**
   - Preheat your oven to 425°F (220°C).
7. **Prepare for Baking:**
   - Optionally, sprinkle sesame seeds on top of the loaf for added flavor and texture.
8. **Bake:**
   - Bake for 30-35 minutes, or until the bread is golden brown and sounds hollow when tapped on the bottom.
9. **Cool:**
   - Let the bread cool on a wire rack before slicing.

Pane Siciliano's crispy crust and tender crumb make it perfect for serving with cheese, meats, or just enjoying with a drizzle of olive oil. Buon appetito!

Herb Focaccia

Ingredients:

For the Dough:

- 3 cups all-purpose flour
- 1 packet (2¼ tsp) active dry yeast
- 1½ cups warm water (110°F or 45°C)
- ¼ cup extra virgin olive oil (plus extra for drizzling)
- 1 tbsp honey or sugar
- 1½ tsp salt

For Topping:

- 2 tbsp fresh rosemary, chopped (or 1 tbsp dried rosemary)
- 1 tbsp fresh thyme leaves (or 1 tsp dried thyme)
- 2-3 cloves garlic, minced (optional)
- Coarse sea salt, for sprinkling
- Additional olive oil, for drizzling

Instructions:

1. **Activate the Yeast:**
   - Dissolve honey or sugar in warm water. Sprinkle yeast over and let sit for 5-10 minutes until frothy.
2. **Mix the Dough:**
   - In a large bowl, combine flour and salt.
   - Add the yeast mixture and olive oil. Mix until a dough forms.
3. **Knead:**
   - Turn the dough onto a floured surface and knead for about 8 minutes until smooth and elastic.
4. **First Rise:**
   - Place dough in a lightly oiled bowl, cover, and let rise in a warm place for 1-1½ hours, or until doubled in size.
5. **Prepare the Pan:**
   - Preheat your oven to 425°F (220°C).
   - Grease a 9x13-inch baking pan or sheet pan with olive oil.
6. **Shape the Dough:**
   - Punch down the dough and transfer it to the prepared pan. Use your fingers to press and stretch the dough to fit the pan, creating dimples all over the surface.
7. **Add Toppings:**
   - Drizzle the top with additional olive oil.

- Sprinkle with chopped rosemary, thyme, minced garlic (if using), and coarse sea salt.
8. **Second Rise:**
    - Let the dough rise in the pan for about 20-30 minutes, or until slightly puffed.
9. **Bake:**
    - Bake for 20-25 minutes, or until the focaccia is golden brown and crisp around the edges.
10. **Cool:**
    - Let the focaccia cool in the pan for a few minutes before transferring it to a wire rack to cool completely.

Herb Focaccia is delightful on its own or with a side of olive oil and balsamic vinegar. It's perfect as a starter, a side for soups and salads, or just as a delicious snack!

Pain au Levain

Ingredients:

For the Levain:

- ¼ cup (60g) active sourdough starter (100% hydration)
- ½ cup (120g) water
- ½ cup (60g) all-purpose flour

For the Dough:

- 1¼ cups (300g) water
- 2½ cups (315g) all-purpose flour
- 1 cup (120g) whole wheat flour
- 1¼ tsp salt
- All of the prepared levain

Instructions:

1. **Prepare the Levain:**
   - Mix the sourdough starter, water, and flour in a bowl. Cover and let sit at room temperature for 8-12 hours, or until bubbly and doubled in size.
2. **Mix the Dough:**
   - In a large bowl, combine the all-purpose flour, whole wheat flour, and salt.
   - Add the levain and water. Mix until the dough starts to come together.
3. **Knead:**
   - Turn the dough onto a floured surface and knead for about 8-10 minutes until smooth and elastic. The dough should be slightly sticky.
4. **First Rise:**
   - Place the dough in a lightly oiled bowl, cover, and let rise for 4-6 hours at room temperature, or until doubled in size. Alternatively, you can let it rise overnight in the refrigerator for a slower, more developed flavor.
5. **Pre-shape:**
   - Turn the dough onto a lightly floured surface and shape it into a loose round. Let it rest for 20-30 minutes.
6. **Shape:**
   - Shape the dough into a round or oval loaf. Place it on a piece of parchment paper or a well-floured proofing basket.
7. **Second Rise:**
   - Cover the dough and let it rise for 1-2 hours, or until it has noticeably puffed up.
8. **Preheat Oven:**

- Preheat your oven to 450°F (230°C). If you have a Dutch oven, place it in the oven while it preheats.
9. **Score and Bake:**
    - Carefully transfer the dough onto a piece of parchment paper (if using a Dutch oven, place the parchment paper with the dough into the Dutch oven).
    - Score the top of the loaf with a sharp knife or bread lame.
    - Bake for 30-35 minutes, or until the bread is deeply browned and sounds hollow when tapped on the bottom.
10. **Cool:**
    - Let the bread cool on a wire rack before slicing.

Pain au Levain has a delightful tangy flavor and a chewy crumb with a crisp crust. Enjoy this artisanal bread fresh or toasted, with your favorite spreads or as part of a hearty meal.

www.ingramcontent.com/pod-product-compliance
Lightning Source LLC
LaVergne TN
LVHW081616060526
838201LV00054B/2272